SCENE BY SCENE COMPARATIVE WORKBOOKS

A DOLL'S HOUSE
by Henrik Ibsen

Cultural Context

Literary Genre

General Vision and Viewpoint

Copyright © 2015 by Amy Farrell.

All rights reserved. No part of this publication may be reproduced, distributed or transmitted in any form or by any means, including photocopying, recording, or other electronic or mechanical methods, without the prior written permission of the publisher, except in the case of brief quotations embodied in critical reviews and certain other noncommercial uses permitted by copyright law. For permission requests, write to the publisher, addressed "Attention: Permissions Coordinator," at the address below.

Scene by Scene
11 Millfield, Enniskerry
Wicklow, Ireland.
www.scenebysceneguides.com

Ordering Information:
Quantity sales. Special discounts are available on quantity purchases by corporations, associations, and others. For details, contact the "Special Sales Department" at the address above.

A Doll's House Comparative Workbook HL16 Amy Farrell. —1st ed.
ISBN 978-1-910949-04-7

2016 Higher Level Comparative Workbook

'A Doll's House' by Henrik Ibsen

The modes at Higher Level for 2016 are:

Cultural Context

This mode refers to the world of the text.

Consider social norms, beliefs, values and attitudes. Think about the roles of men and women and the power structures in this world, etc.

The General Vision and Viewpoint

This mode refers to the author's outlook or view of life and how this viewpoint is represented in the text.

Consider whether the text is bright or dark, optimistic or pessimistic, uplifting or bleak, etc.

Literary Genre

This mode refers to the way the story is told.

Consider the manner and style of narration, characterisation, setting, tension, literary techniques, etc.

About This Workbook

Our workbooks are for the Leaving Certificate Comparative Study.

Each workbook is divided into three coloured sections, one for each comparative mode. This makes it easy to identify each mode and make comparisons and contrasts between texts – simply use matching coloured sections of each of your workbooks to identify similarities and differences between texts.

Each coloured section has two parts to it. The first part focuses on the text itself, and asks text-specific questions within that comparative mode. This helps you get familiar with the text and the aspects of the text that are covered by that mode.

The second part of each section focuses on the mode. In this part, you are asked more general, mode-specific questions. You then have to take what you know about the text and apply it to the mode. By doing this you will become very familiar with what each mode involves, and it will help prepare you for writing comparative answers.

Once complete, this workbook will become your set of notes, to revise and study before the exam.

We hope our workbooks help you conquer the comparative!

Best wishes,

The team at Scene by Scene

scenebysceneguides.com
facebook.com/scene-by-scene

A Doll's House by Henrik Ibsen
Cultural Context

A DOLL'S HOUSE - CULTURAL CONTEXT

What do Torvald, Dr. Rank and Krogstad each work as?

What do Nora and Mrs. Linde work as?

KNOW THE TEXT

What differences do you notice in the work roles of men and women?

Are the Helmers poor or wealthy?

A DOLL'S HOUSE - CULTURAL CONTEXT

Are other characters poor or wealthy?

How does Torvald treat his wife?

KNOW THE TEXT

How does Torvald view women?

How does Nora view the role of women?

A DOLL'S HOUSE - CULTURAL CONTEXT

How was Nora treated by her father?

Do Nora and Torvald have a good marriage?

KNOW THE TEXT

What was Nora's crime?

Do you think Nora is a criminal?

A DOLL'S HOUSE - CULTURAL CONTEXT

Why does Nora lie to her husband, Torvald?

What does Torvald's reaction to his wife's crime, tell you about his priorities?

KNOW THE TEXT

What does Mrs. Linde's relationship with Krogstad show you about the world of this text?

What do Nora and Torvald value?

A DOLL'S HOUSE - CULTURAL CONTEXT

Why is it so shocking when Nora walks out at the end?

KNOW THE MODE

Is **religion** important in this world? What makes you say this?

A DOLL'S HOUSE - CULTURAL CONTEXT

Are **wealth** and **class** important in this world? What view do characters have towards **money**?

KNOW THE MODE

Do the characters in this text hold **traditional beliefs**?

A DOLL'S HOUSE - CULTURAL CONTEXT

Is **race** important in this world?

KNOW THE MODE

Are characters **moral** and **upstanding** in this text?

A DOLL'S HOUSE - CULTURAL CONTEXT

What do people **value** in this text? (What is important to them? What motivates them to act as they do?)

KNOW THE MODE

What kind of **society** do you see in the text? (How do people treat one another? What do they believe in?)

A DOLL'S HOUSE - CULTURAL CONTEXT

Is **family** important in the world of this text?

Is **family** important in the world of this text?

KNOW THE MODE

How are **women** viewed and treated in this story?

A DOLL'S HOUSE - CULTURAL CONTEXT

How are **children** viewed and treated in this story?

KNOW THE MODE

Is **friendship/love** important in this world or are characters self-centred and self-serving? (Is it a warm/loving place or a cold/unloving place?)

A DOLL'S HOUSE - CULTURAL CONTEXT

Is there **conflict** or **violence** in this world? Where do you see it?

Is there **conflict** or **violence** in this world? Where do you see it?

KNOW THE MODE

Is this a **secure** or **dangerous** world?

A DOLL'S HOUSE - CULTURAL CONTEXT

In this world, do characters **conform** or make their own choices **freely?**

KNOW THE MODE

Would you like to live in the world of the text? Use examples to support the points you make.

A DOLL'S HOUSE - CULTURAL CONTEXT

Identify the **key moments** in the play that illustrate the Cultural Context of the text.

KNOW THE MODE

A DOLL'S HOUSE - CULTURAL CONTEXT

What **similarities** do you notice in the Cultural Context of this text and your other comparative texts?

KNOW THE MODE

A DOLL'S HOUSE - CULTURAL CONTEXT

What **differences** do you notice in the Cultural Context of this text and your other comparative texts?.

KNOW THE MODE

KNOW THE MODE

A DOLL'S HOUSE - CULTURAL CONTEXT

A Doll's House by Henrik Ibsen
Literary Genre

How is the story told? (Consider the play format – divided by Acts, spoken dialogue etc.)

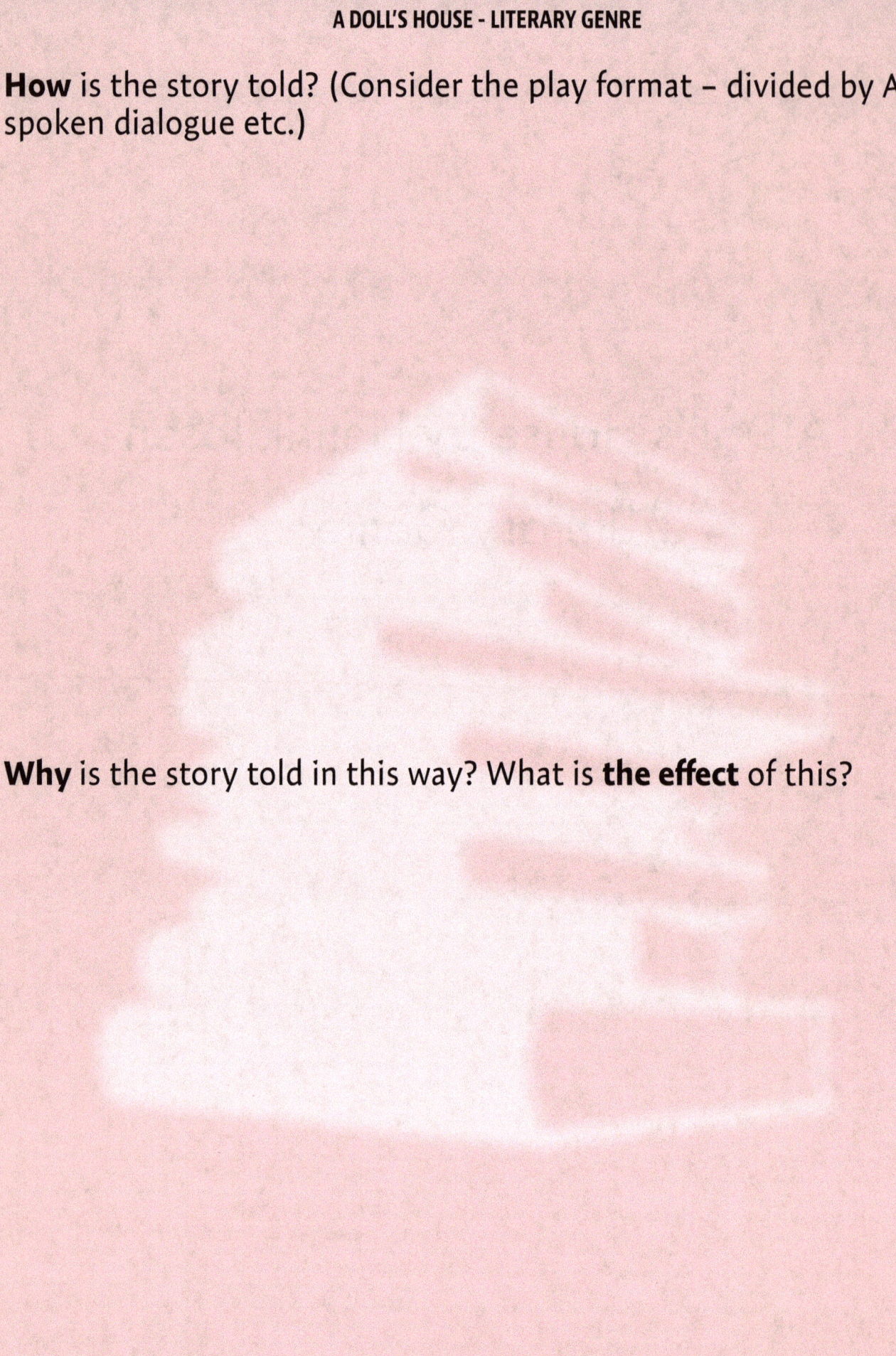

Why is the story told in this way? What is **the effect** of this?

KNOW THE TEXT

What was your **initial view** of **Nora**?

How does Ibsen **develop Nora's character**?

A DOLL'S HOUSE - LITERARY GENRE

Which version of Nora do you prefer? Explain your choice.

How does Ibsen show us Torvald's selfish, childish side?

What is the purpose of Krogstad in the story? (What role does he play?)

What is the purpose of Mrs. Linde in the story? (What role does she play?)

What is the purpose of Dr. Rank in the story? (What role does he play?)

Which characters do you **like**? What makes them appealing?

KNOW THE TEXT

Which characters do you **dislike**? What makes them unappealing?

Is this a play about duty and identity or something else?

What major themes can you identify?

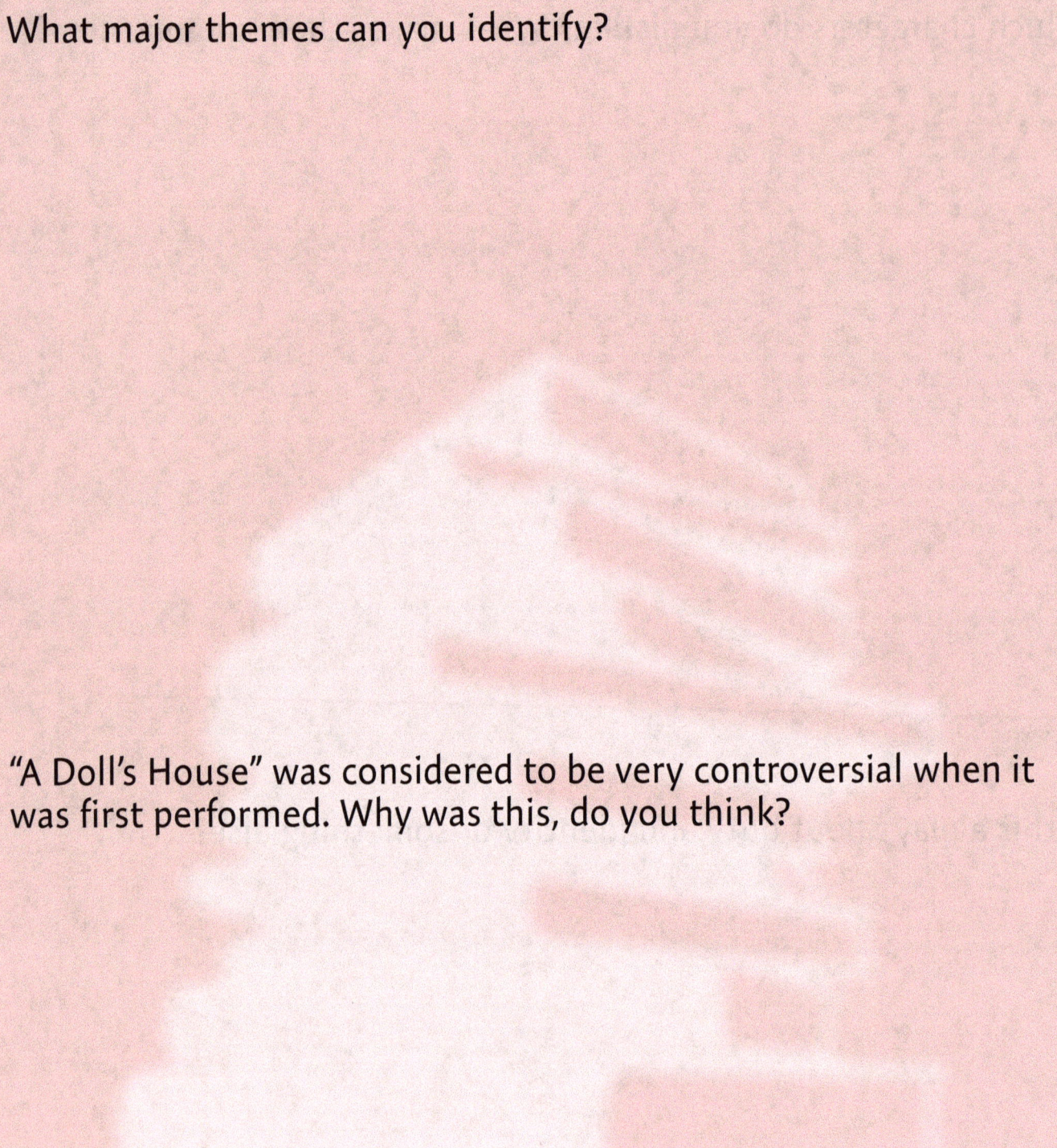

"A Doll's House" was considered to be very controversial when it was first performed. Why was this, do you think?

Did **you** enjoy the **storyline** of the text? (Was it exciting/ compelling/ tense/emotional? Why/why not?)

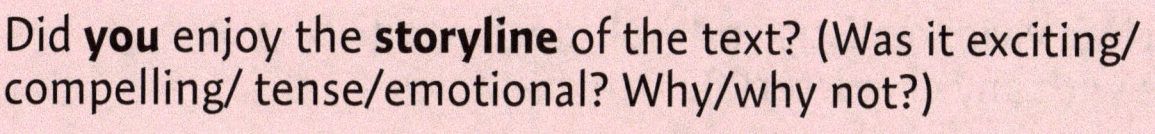

Is there just one **plot** or many plots? How do these relate/what connections can you make between the storylines?

Are **characters** vivid, realistic and well-developed? Do **you** empathise with any character(s)? Use examples.

Did **you** become involved in this story/care about the characters?

KNOW THE MODE

Who was your **favourite character**? What aspects of this character did you enjoy?

Who was your **least favourite character**? What aspects of this character did you dislike?

KNOW THE MODE

Is the story humorous or tragic, romantic or realistic? Explain.

To what **genre** does it belong? Is it Romance, Thriller, Social Realism, Saga, Historical, Fantasy, Science-fiction, Satire, etc.?

How does the playwright create **tension**, **suspense, high emotion** and **excitement** in the text? What literary techniques does he use to good advantage?

KNOW THE MODE

Consider the playwright's use of **tension** and **resolution** in the play. What are the major **tensions/problems/conflicts** in the text? Are they **resolved** or not?

How does the playwright make points to his audience/force us to think/ introduce themes?

Did the playwright make use of any striking patterns of **imagery** or **symbols** to add to the story?

KNOW THE MODE

What is the **climax** (high point) of the story? How do you respond to it?

Comment on the **language** of the play.

KNOW THE MODE

Comment on the **setting** of the play.

Was anything about this play **moving** or **emotional**? How did this emotion add to the story?

Did you enjoy the **ending**? What was satisfying/unsatisfying about it?

A DOLL'S HOUSE - LITERARY GENRE

The experiences of encountering a play (performed), reading a novel and viewing a film are very different. What aspects of the **play form** worked well in this story, in your opinion? Was **this way** of telling the story **successful** and **enjoyable**? What did **you like** about the **way this story was told**? Mention aspects of literary technique that **you** found appealing and enjoyable. (Make use of personal response – your reaction to key moments)

KNOW THE MODE

A DOLL'S HOUSE - LITERARY GENRE

Identify **key moments** in the play that illustrate Literary Genre (the way the story is told). Clearly define literary techniques in your analysis.

KNOW THE MODE

A DOLL'S HOUSE - LITERARY GENRE

What **similarities** do you notice in the Literary Genre of this play and your other comparative texts?

KNOW THE MODE

What **differences** do you notice in the Literary Genre of this play and your other comparative texts?

KNOW THE MODE

A DOLL'S HOUSE - LITERARY GENRE

A DOLL'S HOUSE - LITERARY GENRE

A Doll's House by Henrik Ibsen
General Vision and Viewpoint

A DOLL'S HOUSE - GENERAL VISION AND VIEWPOINT

Do Nora and Torvald love and support each other?

Is Nora under a lot of pressure in this play?

KNOW THE TEXT

How do you feel about the fact that she had to conceal so much from her husband?

What reaction did Nora wish for from her husband when she revealed her misdeed? Did she get the reaction she hoped for?

Were you disappointed by Torvald's reaction? Explain your response.

What does Torvald's reaction to Nora's crime reveal about the playwright's outlook?

KNOW THE TEXT

Were you hopeful about the play's ending, or did you dread the outcome?

What was your reaction to Krogstad's threats?

Are characters in this play happy and content or dissatisfied with life? Consider each character's perspective.

Does Ibsen offer a positive view of love and marriage?

KNOW THE TEXT

Is Nora's future promising, as the play ends?

Is Torvald's future promising?

How does the closing section make you feel?

Did you anticipate a happy ending? Explain.

KNOW THE TEXT

What is Henrik Ibsen telling us about life in this story?

Is his outlook positive or negative, in your view?

Identify bright/hopeful/optimistic moments, or aspects of the play.

KNOW THE MODE

Identify dark/hopeless/pessimistic moments, or aspects of the play.

Is this text **optimistic** or **pessimistic**? Explain.

KNOW THE MODE

What **aspects of life** does the playwright concentrate on? Why does he do this?

A DOLL'S HOUSE - GENERAL VISION AND VIEWPOINT

What **comments** do characters make on their **society** and the problems they're facing?

KNOW THE MODE

Are characters happy or unhappy?

A DOLL'S HOUSE - GENERAL VISION AND VIEWPOINT

What makes characters in this story happy and fulfilled?

KNOW THE MODE

What makes characters in this story unhappy and unfulfilled?

Are **relationships** destructive or nurturing?

What do they reveal about life as we see characters supported/thwarted in their efforts to grow/mature?

KNOW THE MODE

Are **imagery** and **language** bright or dark in the text? (tone of the text)

A DOLL'S HOUSE - GENERAL VISION AND VIEWPOINT

What is the **mood** of this text?

KNOW THE MODE

Did you notice the use of symbolism to add to mood or atmosphere anywhere in the text?

A DOLL'S HOUSE - GENERAL VISION AND VIEWPOINT

What does this story teach us about life?

KNOW THE MODE

What **view of life** is offered in the text?

A DOLL'S HOUSE - GENERAL VISION AND VIEWPOINT

How do you **feel** as you view the play?

KNOW THE MODE

How do you **feel** at the **end**?

Are **questions** raised by the text **resolved** by the end? Are they resolved **happily** or **unhappily**?

KNOW THE MODE

Are *you* **hopeful** or **despairing** regarding the prospects for human **happiness** in this story?

On a scale of one to ten (with one being "most optimistic" and ten being "most pessimistic"), where would you place this text? Explain your choice.

Identify the **key moments** in the play that illustrate the General Vision and Viewpoint of the text.

KNOW THE MODE

A DOLL'S HOUSE - GENERAL VISION AND VIEWPOINT

What **similarities** do you notice in the General Vision and Viewpoint of this text and your other comparative texts?

KNOW THE MODE

A DOLL'S HOUSE - GENERAL VISION AND VIEWPOINT

What **differences** do you notice in the General Vision and Viewpoint of this text and your other comparative texts?

KNOW THE MODE